Dear God,

Jean Ann Shirey

Dear God,

Written by Jean Ann Shirey

Photography by Ted Foley • Consulting Editor: Caitlin Smith Waits

©2018 Jean Ann Shirey, Lamb's Ear Publishing

Library of Congress Control Number: 2018913882
ISBN: 9780997985573

Scripture taken from the NEW AMERICAN STANDARD BIBLE®, ©1960, 1962, 1963, 1968, 1971, 1972, 1973, 1975, 1977, 1995 by The Lockman Foundation. Used by permission. www.Lockman.org. All photographs were taken in Hawaii, except for photo on page 4 taken by Jean Ann Shirey at the request of Jesus' beloved, Mary Alice Wise.

37 Now on the last day, the great *day* of the feast,
Jesus stood and cried out, saying,
"If anyone is thirsty, let him come to Me and drink.

38 He who believes in Me, as the Scripture said,
'From his innermost being will flow rivers of living water.'"

John 7:37, 38

Introduction

Dear God,
Please let Your love,
which You freely gave
through Your Son, Jesus,
to me and to the world,
be returned to You
by the power of the Holy Spirit
with gratitude, so
You are loved, honored
and obeyed joyfully
as You deserve
by me, my family, friends,
and as many as You choose
to bring to You through us.
May we be a huge group
who really loves You back
and are of loving,
useful service to You
according to Your will.

Dear God,
You are the heart
of my beat,
the drum of my soul's
eternal reverberations,
and the calling
of my essence.
Creator of all
by tethered line
to daily decisions.
Walking home toward You
in the Name of Jesus.

¹ In the beginning was the Word,
and the Word was with God,
and the Word was God.
² He was in the beginning with God.

³ All things came into being through Him,
and apart from Him nothing came into being
that has come into being.

⁴ In Him was life,
and the life was the light of men.

⁵ The light shines in the darkness,
and the darkness did not comprehend it.
John 1:1-5

Dear God,
Onward through the tall and pine trees,
upward through the rolling mist,
streams of light from heaven beaming
flow through darkened needle tips.

And I in Eden, weep at hearts
so swayed by Satan's lie.
What to do, LORD, what to do?
Is to love and accept, approval,
or to take a stand too harsh?
Shall I be judged for saying nothing?
So, I watch and wonder.
Please guide me, Lord.
I stand aside and watch
sunrise through pine trees.

You so freely loved sinners,
and they changed.
I love, and they want me
to go along with what You say is wrong.

Out of Eden fallen,
take me home to my abode
so rickety with my brain-idled dear,
where peace of mind returns.
I run home when I see,
glad to joy of my own burdens swept.

But, I've still loved the pines,
so close to kiss Your face,
and I touch their fallen seeds.
I also from earth, raise my face
in the hope of Your kiss.

²¹ So Peter seeing him *said to Jesus, "Lord, and what about this man?".

²² Jesus said to him, "If I want him to remain until I come, what *is that* to you? You follow Me!"

John 21:21, 22

¹³ Joshua went to him and said to him, "Are you for us or for our adversaries?"

¹⁴ He said, "No; rather I indeed come now as captain of the host of the Lord." And Joshua fell on his face to the earth, and bowed down, and said to him, "What has my lord to say to his servant?"

Joshua 5:13b, 14

¹⁵ And he said to them, "Go into all the world and preach the gospel to all creation.

¹⁶ He who has believed and has been baptized shall be saved; but he who has disbelieved shall be condemned.

Mark 16:15, 16

Dear God,
Soul of joy
sweetest tended
by Your love
for me amended
to cover my nakedness,
so I could cover
my brother
in a blanket
of love,
not rail
head-shaking,
but love's
own beautiful
garment,
Yours to me
and mine to Thee.

Dear God,
The wonders of beautiful delights
and breath drenching agony
are pulsating simultaneously.

Please help me to experience this with You
not to miss my life, or push it away.
You are my life.

Please hold my hand.

**[7] Then the LORD God formed man of dust from the ground,
and breathed into his nostrils the breath of life;
and man became a living being.**

Genesis 2:7

**[6] Jesus said to him, "I am the way, the truth, and the life;
no one comes to the Father but through Me."**

John 14:6

Dearest,

Teach me Your heart.

Your word I have treasured in my heart,
That I may not sin against You.

Psalm 119:11

Let the words of my mouth and the meditation of my heart
Be acceptable in Your sight,
O LORD, my rock and my Redeemer.

Psalm 19:14

Dear God,

Rare beauty of mine,

I just love You with my heart.

Rare beauty of my heart,

I just love You back.

19 We love, because He first loved us.

1 John 4:19

22 And when He had said this, He breathed on them and said to them, "Receive the Holy Spirit.

John 20:22

Pure Love and Joy,

Help me walk on Your water.

You are my life-giving force.

Thank You for taking me

wherever we are going.

[28] **Peter said to Him, "Lord, if it is You, command me to come to You on the water."**

[29] **And He said, "Come!" And Peter got out of the boat, and walked on the water and came toward Jesus.**

Matthew 14:28, 29

Dear God,

I feel like a flickering little candle.

You steady my flame with Your quietness.

Your calm voice settles my soul.

You not only are Light, but

You combine to be the Light in me.

I have many questions,

and You hone in on me to give direction.

Please help me turn for Your directions.

Help me to live Your way.

Please forgive my fearful stubbornness.

Word, speak steadily over me and the household
of faith.

In the Almighty name of Jesus, I pray.
Amen.

"These things I have spoken to you so that you may be kept from stumbling."

John 16:1

Dear God,

You are very pleasing

and kind to me!

Am I pleasing You?

**²² and whatever we ask we receive from Him,
because we keep His commandments and do the things
that are pleasing in His sight.**

1 John 3:22

**For the Lᴏʀᴅ takes pleasure in His people;
He will beautify the afflicted ones with salvation.**

Psalm 149:4

This morning I heard:

"Trust Me. I am leading you."

God your Father

Dear Father,

Thank You. I will.

Love,

²⁷ My sheep hear My voice, and I know them, and they follow Me;
²⁸ and I give eternal life to them, and they will never perish;
and no one will snatch them out of My hand.

John 10:27, 28

¹⁵ 'I know your deeds, that you are neither cold nor hot;
I wish that you were cold or hot.

¹⁶ So because you are lukewarm, and neither hot nor cold,
I will spit you out of My mouth.

Revelation 3:15,16

²⁰ Behold, I stand at the door and knock; if anyone hears My voice and opens the door, I will come in to him and will dine with him, and he with Me.

Revelation 3:20

The LORD appeared to him from afar, *saying*,
"I have loved you with an everlasting love;
Therefore I have drawn you with lovingkindness.

Jeremiah 31:3

Dear God,
I see my family—children, grandchildren,
and I know the passion, the longing
that sparked their lives.

Do we still have the spark?
When I speak about You to someone else,
my voice still cracks with emotion.
You loved me first,
but I love You back.

[19] Go therefore and make disciples of all the nations,
baptizing them in the name of the Father and the Son and the Holy Spirit,
[20] teaching them to observe all that I commanded you;
and lo, I am with you always, even to the end of the age."
Matthew 28:19, 20

Dear God,

Please do not let me talk to You and not talk to others about You.

Do not let me talk to others about You and not talk to You.

You are the balance on the beam, and I praise Your name.

Blessed be the Name of Jesus, Who was and is and is to come.

Savior, Redeemer, Wonder of my soul, glorify Your Holy Name.

May Your praise sing out.

May Your name ring forever in joy from the lips of Your servants.

Please let me and my family live in service to You.

Please give us the gifts of love, faithfulness, and obedience to You that we might serve You to Your coming and then forever.

I love You. Please hold me close. You are my forever love.

In the name of Jesus, I pray. Amen.

Dear God,
I come to You
and sit beside You
with the hope of joy.

A joyful heart is good medicine,
But a broken spirit dries up the bones.

Proverbs 17:22

[22] Therefore you too have grief now; but I will see you again,
and your heart will rejoice,
and no one *will* take your joy away from you.

John 16:22

[8] For by grace you have been saved through faith; and that not of yourselves,

it is the gift of God;

[9] not as a result of works, so that no one may boast.

[10] For we are His workmanship, created in Christ Jesus for good works,

which God prepared beforehand so that we would walk in them.

Ephesians 2:8-10

[27] Peace I leave with you;

My peace I give to you; not as the world gives do I give to you.

Do not let your heart be troubled, nor let it be fearful.

John 14:27 * (Page 31)

Dear God,
I talk when I should listen
and listen when I should speak up.
At times, I am anxious and backwards.
Sometimes nothing feels right.
I am confused and frustrated.
Where do I get off this train?
When I cannot seem to hold Your hand,
I grab for Your coat tail,
like skaters flying by on a chain.
I grab on and am flung through life.
Life, death, sickness, challenges,
they come if I am ready or not.
I am not ready for this today.
It comes.
I am ready.
It comes.

Life just is:
busy, rolling tide.
It comes,
      and it goes.
Where am I?
  Who?
You are my center point.
"My peace I give to you;
not as the world gives, do I give to you." *

I try so hard to do what is right.
You tell me not to try so hard.
You do through me
what I cannot do myself.

You are in me, and I am in You.
You promised. I know it is true.
You are my quiet, the keeper of my soul.

¹⁷ The Spirit and the bride say, "Come." And let the one who hears say, "Come." And let the one who is thirsty come; let the one who wishes take the water of life without cost.

Revelation 22:17

Dear God,
Let me come with joy,
naked, just as I am.

Carry me over the threshold.

I am safe in the arms of Jesus.
Home, I am home!
Light lifting, love beaming,
sparkling Spirit around,
rays through me. Life. Truth.
Family. Home. Ahhh!
I am home in the name of Jesus.

[24] "Truly, truly, I say to you,
he who hears My word,
and believes Him who sent Me,
has eternal life,
and does not come into judgment,
but has passed out of death into life.

John 5:24

Dear God,
I am sitting here loving
and adoring You with my heart,
sincerely appreciating
all the love and goodness
You put into my life.
This world is incredible,
and I watch it in awe,
remembering You.

Still, what I love most is You.
So, I look at You-
waiting for Your touch,
listening for Your voice—willing.
You surround me, and I love it.
All I can do is notice and appreciate You.

The interaction between us
is the deepest of my life.
Nothing else matches the love and joy You bring.
I am so glad You asked me to come.

Dear God,

My relationship with You

is all about love and trust.

⁶ Therefore humble yourselves under the mighty hand of God,

that He may exalt you at the proper time,

⁷ casting all your anxiety on Him, because He cares for you.

1 Peter 5:6,7

Dear God,

Please give me eyes to see Your goodness

and a heart to see Your love.

You have prepared a beautiful plan for overcoming,

for new creation if You will.

Pruning branches,

being cut out of life as preparation for new growth

in another direction.

I love You as the Master Gardener of my being.

My soul looks forward to You,

tender shoots guided by dear love.

"I am the true vine, and My Father is the vinedresser.

2 Every branch in Me that does not bear fruit, He takes away;

and every *branch* that bears fruit, He prunes it so that it may bear more fruit.

John 15:1,2

²⁴ Jesus presented another parable to them, saying,

"The kingdom of heaven may be compared
to a man who sowed good seed in his field.

²⁵ But while his men were sleeping,
his enemy came and sowed tares among the wheat, and went away.

²⁶ But when the wheat sprouted and bore grain, then the tares became evident also.

²⁷ The slaves of the landowner came and said to him,
'Sir, did you not sow good seed in your field? How then does it have tares?'

²⁸ And he said to them, 'An enemy has done this!'

The slaves *said to him, 'Do you want us, then, to go and gather them up?'

²⁹ But he *said, 'No; for while you are gathering up the tares,
you may uproot the wheat with them.

³⁰ Allow both to grow together until the harvest; and in the time of the harvest
I will say to the reapers,

"First gather up the tares and bind them in bundles to burn them up;
but gather the wheat into my barn."'"

Matthew 13:24-30

Dear God,

The first thing I saw was a humming bird,

Round-bellied, grey-green, eating from the feeder.

There are three peace roses outside the window,

two open wide, the third in medium bloom.

How could You have blessed me so?

Poppies and roses came this year by Your hand.

A neighborhood boy came to help clear away the thistles.

We all grow together on this earth.

The blooms, the fruit, the thistles,

we are all here becoming more of who we were when we answered Your call.

It seems easier in my garden.

I was my own grass puller, weed plucker, and thistle stomper.

I used gloves, bagged neatly, and threw away.

Now, I ask the boy next door to do it, directing.

But here in this world of my living garden,
You tell us to love the weeds, grass in the flower beds, and thistles.
You tell me I do not love You, if I do not love, even when they scratch.
I am walking wounded, scars in place.
You are Healing Balm, Courage Extraordinary.
You use my pollen to miraculously make thistles into fruit trees,
flowering beautiful, spreading fruit.

I watch You work,
You wore the first thorns.

Love in Christ by Resurrection Power,

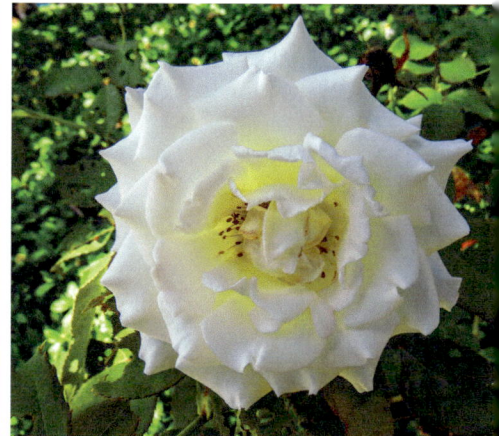

[24] "Therefore everyone who hears these words of Mine and acts on them, may be compared to a wise man who built his house on the rock.

Matthew 7:24

Dear God,

In a lifetime,

I will still be working on Your Beatitudes.

I really want to love. Please help me

and my generations to be loving people.

When Jesus saw the crowds, He went up on the mountain;

and after He sat down, His disciples came to Him.

2 He opened His mouth and *began* to teach them, saying,

3 "Blessed are the poor in spirit, for theirs is the kingdom of heaven.

4 "Blessed are those who mourn, for they shall be comforted.

5 "Blessed are the gentle, for they shall inherit the earth.

6 "Blessed are those who hunger and thirst for righteousness, for they shall be satisfied.

7 "Blessed are the merciful, for they shall receive mercy.

8 "Blessed are the pure in heart, for they shall see God.

Matthew 5:1-8

² The angel of the Lord appeared to him in a blazing fire from the midst of a bush;
and he looked, and behold, the bush was burning with fire,
yet the bush was not consumed.

Exodus 3:2

Numbers 3:4

¹¹ "As for me, I baptize you with water for repentance,
but He who is coming after me is mightier than I,
and I am not fit to remove His sandals; He will baptize you with the Holy Spirit and fire.

Matthew 3:11

³ And there appeared to them tongues as of fire distributing themselves,
and they rested on each one of them.

Acts 2:3

¹⁰ Jesus answered and said to her, "If you knew the gift of God,
and who it is who says to you, 'Give Me a drink,'
you would have asked Him, and He would have given you living water."

John 4:10

Dear God,

Let the fire of love burn in us, Lord Jesus.

Extinguish wrong doing. Pull us back from evil burning.

Please put the passion of Christ,

the Loving Holy flames of pure Spirit devotion, in our hearts.

Let loving, life-giving water overflow from each of us.

Regard my family and the family of the saints according to Your will for the chosen people of God in Christ.

Let us fulfill Your calling to reach others in love and lift up the name of Jesus.

According to Your will and word, let it be done.

I love You forever,

my heart in Christ.

The Lord is my shepherd; I shall not want.

² He maketh me to lie down in green pastures:

he leadeth me beside the still waters.

³ He restoreth my soul:

he leadeth me in the paths of righteousness for his name's sake.

⁴ Yea, though I walk through the valley of the shadow of death, I will fear no evil:

for thou art with me;

thy rod and thy staff they comfort me.

⁵ Thou preparest a table before me in the presence of mine enemies:

thou anointest my head with oil;

my cup runneth over.

⁶ Surely goodness and mercy shall follow me all the days of my life:

and I will dwell in the house of the Lord forever.

Psalm 23, King James Version

Dear God,

I am restless.

Your destiny for so many has been the ultimate sacrifice for my well-being.

How can this be that you love me so?

My whole generation is alive and has the opportunity to truly be alive in Christ,

because You chose us.

In this confusion called sin,

You brought love, peace, and order

through Your Son, Jesus, by sacrifice.

How can this be?

How can You take such a great step for me?

When I seek to be a loving person, my lack of love is ever before my eyes.

The prideful spirit, temperamental ways, and self-seeking stare back at me more glaringly,

because I seek to be Your reflection in the dark world that mirrors and mocks my own carnality.

How can it be?

I wonder and ponder,

unable to grasp in my mind what Your Spirit sings in my heart.

You love me.

You "restoreth my soul."

You "leadeth me in the path of righteousness."

I know that I know;

You are a good God, faithful, kind, and true.

Many have faced ridicule, sacrificed, and died, so I can know Your love.

Oh God, what is my destiny in You?

Resurrection power, please overflow with love, mercy, and forgiveness

in this cup at Your table.

Make this family true to Your calling by Your might.

You are my truest love.

You came for me.

You sent Your army to my rescue.

Please let me live for You.

Let each day be marked as if my last.

I can overlook a lot others say and do, if this is my last day.

You bring me wonder-filled appreciation.

Your plans are my heart's desire.

I want so to fulfill Your destiny for my life.

I want my family to be in Your will.

I want my church, Lord; my city;

state; country; the world, Lord; and all Your people to stand and love You.

You are the life in us.

Please let our lives revolve around pleasing You.

Joy in our soul,

let love and obedience follow.

"Here am I! Send me."

⁸ Also I heard the voice of the Lord, saying,
Whom shall I send, and who will go for us?
Then said I, Here am I; send me.
Isaiah 6:8

20 Brethren, do not be children in your thinking; yet in evil be infants,

but in your thinking be mature.

1 Corinthians 14:20

3 (Now the man Moses was very humble, more than any man

who was on the face of the earth.)

Numbers 12:3

29 Take My yoke upon you and learn from Me, for I am gentle and humble in heart,

and YOU WILL FIND REST FOR YOUR SOULS.

30 For My yoke is easy and My burden is light."

Matthew 11:29, 30

13 But now faith, hope, love, abide these three; but the greatest of these is love.

1 Corinthians 13:13

Dear God,
Why am I not a more mature Christian?
My love and obedience lack so much.
Please help me, my family,
and the family of people who believe in You
be humble and loving through Your power.
In the Almighty name of Your Son, Jesus, I pray.
Amen.

Dear God,

I just want to listen to You.

I love You.

⁰ When you are in distress and all these things have come upon you, in the latter days you will return to the Lᴏʀᴅ your God and listen to His voice.

Deuteronomy 4:30

¹⁸ So take care how you listen; for whoever has, to him *more* shall be given; and whoever does not have, even what he thinks he has shall be taken away from him."

Luke 8:18

³⁵ Then a voice came out of the cloud, saying, "This is My Son, *My* Chosen One; listen to Him!"

Luke 9:35

Dear God,
I am so grateful; You told me
all my needs are met.
You have given me
all my greatest heart's desires.
You are my gift. You know.
You are the One who finishes me.
You are my focus, my center point,
my cornerstone.

Delight yourself in the Lord; And He will give you the desires of your heart.
Psalm 37:4

[38] Peter *said* to them, "Repent, and each of you be baptized in the name of Jesus Christ for the forgiveness of your sins; and you will receive the gift of the Holy Spirit.
Acts 2: 38

[20] having been built on the foundation of the apostles and prophets, Christ Jesus Himself being the corner *stone*,
Ephesians 2:20

⁴Or do you think lightly of the riches of His kindness and tolerance and patience, not knowing that the kindness of God leads you to repentance?

Romans 2:4

Good morning Lord,
How are You?
How was Your night and day?
Did you move the stars around?
Did the moonflower open wide?
Did the rose scent fill the air?
Did You watch things creep and crawl?

Did You send the sun's rays over to my eyes again
and make the sky so brilliant that I cried,
wonder-filled with awesome
to watch Your painting in the sky?
Did You bring the cardinals home
and fill the bird songs in the air?
Did you make the rooster crow
and feather hens feet all around?

Could I ever stop writing about all Your many works
from where I sit to sing Your praise
and lift You up?
You are such a pleasure!

Dear God,

Please be the life in me,

the spark of love that fulfills my destiny.

You are my courage, faithful and true.

Please show me Your life and keep me in You.

You are my love, the spark in my eyes.

You are the One who keeps me alive.

You are my thrill, the hope of my way

in the truth of Your word, keep me in You, my life.

In Jesus' name, I pray.

Love,

25 Jesus said to her, "I am the resurrection and the life;
he who believes in Me will live even if he dies,
26 and everyone who lives and believes in Me will never die. Do you believe this?"

John 11: 25: 26

¹¹ Put on the full armor of God, so that you will be able to stand firm against the schemes of the devil.

¹² For our struggle is not against flesh and blood, but against the rulers, against the powers, against the world forces of this darkness, against the spiritual *forces* of wickedness in the heavenly *places*.

¹³ Therefore, take up the full armor of God, so that you will be able to resist in the evil day, and having done everything, to stand firm.

¹⁴ **Stand firm therefore,** HAVING GIRDED YOUR LOINS WITH TRUTH, **and** HAVING PUT ON THE BREASTPLATE OF RIGHTEOUSNESS,

¹⁵ **and having shod** YOUR FEET WITH THE PREPARATION OF THE GOSPEL OF PEACE;

¹⁶ in addition to all, taking up the shield of faith with which you will be able to extinguish all the flaming arrows of the evil *one*.

¹⁷ And take THE HELMET OF SALVATION, and the sword of the Spirit, which is the word of God.

¹⁸ With all prayer and petition pray at all times in the Spirit, and with this in view, be on the alert with all perseverance and petition for all the saints,

¹⁹ and *pray* on my behalf, that utterance may be given to me in the opening of my mouth, to make known with boldness the mystery of the gospel,

²⁰ for which I am an ambassador in chains; that in *proclaiming* it I may speak boldly, as I ought to speak.

Ephesians 6:11-20

Dear God,
Please bless and help my family.
I look to You for tender care
over the wounds and hurts this world gives,
to place the breast plate over us
and the armor You have given
to keep us on Your quest.
I give You my life and family
to keep each one in tender truth
with Your strong arm in faithful love
and all You know.
I love and trust You with my family.

"At that time," declares the Lord, "I will be the God of all the families of Israel, and they shall be My people."

Jeremiah 31:1

Dear God,
You are my love,
and I am Your tender heart.
Together we are one.

20 "I do not ask on behalf of these alone, but for those also who believe in Me through their word;

21 that they may all be one; even as You, Father, *are* in Me and I in You,

that they also may be in Us, so that the world may believe that You sent Me.

22 The glory which You have given Me I have given to them, that they may be one, just as We are one;

23 I in them and You in Me, that they may be perfected in unity,

so that the world may know that You sent Me, and loved them, even as You have loved Me.

John 17:20-23

[11] For the poor will never cease *to be* in the land;

therefore I command you, saying, 'You shall freely open your hand to your brother,

to your needy and poor in your land.'

Deuteronomy 15:11

[42] A poor widow came and put in two small copper coins, which amount to a cent.

[43] Calling His disciples to Him, He said to them,

"Truly I say to you, this poor widow put in more than all the contributors

to the treasury;

[44] for they all put in out of their surplus,

but she, out of her poverty, put in all she owned, all she had to live on."

Mark 12:42-44

[17] This I command you, that you love one another.

John 15:17

Dear God,
Only let me remember You
and Your poor, vulnerable people
when my heart beats
or when I breathe air.

Let me join with others
in Your body to do Your bidding
for You by You with You forever.
Your Bride,

Dear God,

Please forgive me

when I am silent too long,

or when my words fall

on my own deaf ears

because I did not listen to You.

² "I am the Lᴏʀᴅ your God, who brought you out of the land of Egypt, out of the house of slavery. ³ "You shall have no other gods before Me.
Exodus 20:2,3

²⁴ And He was saying to them, "Take care what you listen to. By your standard of measure it will be measured to you; and more will be given you besides.
Mark 4:24

Therefore there is now no condemnation for those who are in Christ Jesus.
Romans 8:1

³⁷ But in all these things we overwhelmingly conquer through Him who loved us.
Romans 8:37

Dear God,
You continue to love and woo me.
This is the greatest wonder of my life.
You love me until I see
and hear You loving me,
because You are always loving me.

16 For God so loved the world, that he gave his only begotten Son, that whosoever believeth in him should not perish, but have everlasting life.

John 3:16 King James Version

36 "Teacher, which is the great commandment in the Law?"

37 And He said to him, "'You shall love the Lord your God with all your heart, and with all your soul,

and with all your mind.' 38 This is the great and foremost commandment.

39 The second is like it, 'You shall love your neighbor as yourself.'

40 On these two commandments depend the whole Law and the Prophets."

Matthew 22:36-40

5 and from Jesus Christ, the faithful witness, the firstborn of the dead, and the ruler of the kings of the earth.

To Him who loves us and released us from our sins by His blood—

Revelation 1:5

Dear God,
My soul and spirit reach up to You,
as Your grace and peace reach down to me.
I fall before You, with love I receive my destiny!
My Lord Jesus!

¹⁶ Now may our Lord Jesus Christ Himself and God our Father,

who has loved us and given us eternal comfort and good hope by grace,

¹⁷ comfort and strengthen your hearts in every good work and word.

2 Thessalonians 2:16,17

Dear God,

Please let me live in truth,

so I can live in You.

I want to honor You.

Love,

^{31} So Jesus was saying to those Jews who had believed Him, "If you continue in My word, *then* you are truly disciples of Mine; ^{32} and you will know the truth, and the truth will make you free."

John 8:31, 32

⁴ Abide in Me, and I in you. As the branch
cannot bear fruit of itself unless it abides
in the vine,
so neither *can* you unless you abide in Me.
⁵ I am the vine, you are the branches;
he who abides in Me and I in him,
he bears much fruit,
for apart from Me you can do nothing.

John 15:4,5

Dear God,
All other love springs
out of the well of Your love for me.
Our relationship is the key.
All other love comes as the fruit
and blessings of our relationship.
I love You!

[34] A new commandment I give to you, that you love one another, even as I have loved you, that you also love one another.
John 13:34

[16] We have come to know and have believed the love which God has for us. God is love, and the one who abides in love abides in God, and God abides in him.
1 John 4:16

Dear God,

Please let Your love light my life into Your day.

My Direction, please pour over me and birth Your Word,

love to generations who are true to You.

Speak to my ears and turn me to You, my Heart.

Love in the Name of Jesus,

⁹ But you are a chosen race, a royal priesthood, a holy nation, a people for *God's* own possession,

so that you may proclaim the excellencies of Him

who has called you out of darkness into His marvelous light;

1 Peter 2:9, 10

Dear God,
You and I were destined to be
a great partnership for good.
Surrender to You is my complete joy.
Pushing You away is my greatest regret.
Thank You for not leaving me in sorrow
and for giving me Your hope.
Thank You for always bringing me home.
Love in the name of Jesus,

**8 Be of sober *spirit*, be on the alert.
Your adversary, the devil, prowls around like a roaring lion,
seeking someone to devour.**

**9 But resist him, firm in *your* faith, knowing that the same experiences of suffering
are being accomplished by your brethren who are in the world.**

**10 After you have suffered for a little while, the God of all grace, who called you
to His eternal glory in Christ, will Himself perfect, confirm,
strengthen *and* establish you.**

11 To Him *be* dominion forever and ever. Amen.

1 Peter 5:8-11

Dear God,

Please let me find You.

Come to me now.

I've tried too hard, too long, and it did not work.

Come to me like smooth water.

Overflow my banks, and let me go with You.

I was made to float on You, in Your arms, holding Your hand, resting in You.

I was made for You, my one true Love.

7 "Ask, and it will be given to you; seek, and you will find; knock, and it will be opened to you.

8 For everyone who asks receives, and he who seeks finds, and to him who knocks it will be opened.

Matthew 7:7, 8

16 "My beloved is mine, and I am his; He pastures *his flock* among the lilies.

Song of Solomon 2:16

Dear God,
You are my Father,
my family name.
Wherever I go, I am created for You.

9 "Pray, then, in this way: 'Our Father who is in heaven, Hallowed be Your name.
Matthew 6:9

44 "The kingdom of heaven is like a treasure hidden in the field,
which a man found and hid *again*;
and from joy over it he goes and sells all that he has and buys that field.
Matthew 13:44

19 Therefore, those also who suffer according to the will of God
shall entrust their souls to a faithful Creator in doing what is right.
1 Peter 4:19

Dear God,

Please forgive me when I am polite,

rather than passionate for You and others.

In the name of Jesus, I pray.

Amen.

**⁴ But I have *this* against you, that you have left your first love.
⁵ Therefore remember from where you have fallen,
and repent and do the deeds you did at first;
or else I am coming to you
and will remove your lampstand out of its place—unless you repent.**

Revelation 2:4,5

¹⁶ **John answered and said to them all, "As for me, I baptize you with water;**
but One is coming who is mightier than I,
and I am not fit to untie the thong of His sandals;
He will baptize you with the Holy Spirit and fire.

Luke 3:16

Dear God,

Brand me with You,

my iron from Heaven,

sent for me.

Dear God,
You are the One who is good, kind, and true.
You are the Bridegroom with Your arms around me
and the gifts you gave me secured.
You are ready to send me into a new day with You,
as Your love guides my heart.
Please help each of my family members, children,
extended family, and friends all around the world in the very same way.
I love You so much.

16 "I, Jesus, have sent My angel to testify to you these things for the churches. I am the root and the descendant of David, the bright morning star." Revelation 22:16

My little children, I am writing these things to you so that you may not sin. And if anyone sins, we have an Advocate with the Father, Jesus Christ the righteous; 2 and He Himself is the propitiation for our sins; and not for ours only, but also for *those of* the whole world.

1 John 2:1-3

Dear God,

You pursue me so hard and with such might,

that it takes my breath just to try to keep up.

3 At one time we too were foolish, disobedient, deceived and enslaved by all kinds of passions and pleasures.
We lived in malice and envy, being hated and hating one another.

4 But when the kindness and love of God our Savior appeared,
5 he saved us, not because of righteous things we had done, but because of his mercy.
He saved us through the washing of rebirth and renewal by the Holy Spirit,
6 whom he poured out on us generously through Jesus Christ our Savior,
7 so that, having been justified by his grace, we might become heirs having the hope of eternal life.
8 This is a trustworthy saying. And I want you to stress these things,

so that those who have trusted in God may be careful to devote themselves to doing what is good.
These things are excellent and profitable for everyone.
14 Our people must also learn to engage in good deeds to meet pressing needs, so that they will not be unfruitful.

Titus 3:3-8, 14

Dear God,

You are complete without me,

but I am not complete without You.

You just choose to want me.

I choose You!

**¹⁴ God said to Moses, "I AM WHO I AM";
and He said, "Thus you shall say to the sons of Israel, 'I AM has sent me to you.'"
¹⁵ God, furthermore, said to Moses, "Thus you shall say to the sons of Israel,
'The Lᴏʀᴅ, the God of your fathers, the God of Abraham, the God of Isaac,
and the God of Jacob,
has sent me to you.' This is My name forever,
and this is My memorial-name to all generations.**

Exodus 3:14, 15

**²¹ She will bear a Son; and you shall call His name Jesus,
for He will save His people from their sins."**

Matthew 1:21

Dear God,

Thank You that Your expression is total, great love.

Please let my expression follow Yours.

This world grabs at my heart.

Just to live is to see so many instances of problems and pain.

I open my eyes to the sorrows and disasters people experience.

My heart quakes; the suffering and evil shake me.

My own sin saddens me.

I do not like a lot of what is here.

It soothes me to know Your name is Emmanuel, God with us.

I think about You being with me a lot.

You make it adequate to be the only person,

because I am never alone with You.

I am always with Jesus.

I have Your favor and smile.

You continue to amaze me with Your love!

I love You in the name of Jesus!

³¹ God saw all that He had made, and behold, it was very good.

And there was evening and there was morning, the sixth day.

Genesis 1:31

²³ for all have sinned and fall short of the glory of God,

Romans 3:23

²² Now all this took place to fulfill what was spoken by the Lord through the prophet:

²³ "BEHOLD, THE VIRGIN SHALL BE WITH CHILD AND SHALL BEAR A SON,

AND THEY SHALL CALL HIS NAME IMMANUEL," which translated means, "GOD WITH US."

Matthew 1: 22, 23

¹⁷ By this, love is perfected with us, so that we may have confidence in the day of judgment; because as He is, so also are we in this world.

¹⁸ There is no fear in love; but perfect love casts out fear, because fear involves punishment, and the one who fears is not perfected in love.

1 John 4:17, 18

Dear God,
Thank You for providing a door from You to me.
Thank You for letting me choose Jesus.
It was You all along.
It has always been You taking care of me,
making something lovely happen.
The sky, the sunset, a kind word, all to let me know You love me,
and I should not give up.
Just thinking about You satisfies me.
You are my calm, peace, and wisdom.
You are the love of my life.

**⁹ I am the door; if anyone enters through Me, he will be saved,
and will go in and out and find pasture.**

John 10:9

**²¹ He who overcomes, I will grant to him to sit down with Me on My throne,
as I also overcame and sat down with My Father on His throne.**

Revelation 3:21

**²² But the fruit of the Spirit is love, joy, peace, patience, kindness, goodness,
faithfulness, ²³ gentleness, self-control; against such things there is no law.**

Galatians 5:22, 23

Consider it all joy, my brethren, when you encounter various trials,

[3] knowing that the testing of your faith produces endurance.

[4] And let endurance have *its* perfect result, so that you may be perfect and complete, lacking in nothing.

[5] But if any of you lacks wisdom, let him ask of God, who gives to all generously and without reproach, and it will be given to him.

James 1:2-5

Dear God,
Please let me remember how much I need You,
especially when I think I can do something
and do not consider to ask for Your specific
guidance and assistance.
Please be first in all of my considerations,
and do not let my heart forget the benefits
of loving You.
I gladly surrender to You!

⁵ Come, house of Jacob, and let us walk in the light of the Lᴏʀᴅ.
Isaiah 2:5

¹⁵ "If you love Me, you will keep My commandments.

**¹⁶ I will ask the Father, and He will give you another Helper,
that He may be with you forever;**

**¹⁷ *that is* the Spirit of truth, whom the world cannot receive,
because it does not see Him or know Him,
but you know Him because He abides with you and will be in you.**

¹⁸ "I will not leave you as orphans; I will come to you.

John 14:15-18

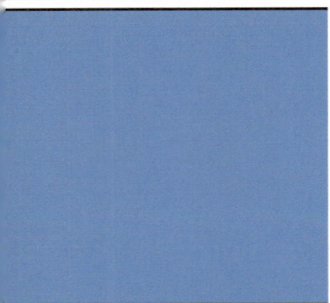

Dear God,

You've painted me with Your brush and lifted Your strokes of color.

With every hue perfectly made, You found the essence of me.

You tenderly laid each layer before me and formed the background with tears.

I wondered when I saw what You had done, the masterpiece of my years.

Each part was right; it all fit so well. I was silent when I saw it all.

The wonder is the Artist, Who bought my life, the Sage of perfection.

I trust You, Age of Life, Song of Art.

13 For You formed my inward parts; You wove me in my mother's womb.
14 I will give thanks to You, for I am fearfully and wonderfully made;
Wonderful are Your works, And my soul knows it very well.
15 My frame was not hidden from You, When I was made in secret,
***And* skillfully wrought in the depths of the earth;**
16 Your eyes have seen my unformed substance; And in Your book were all written
The days that were ordained *for me*, When as yet there was not one of them.

Psalm 139:13-16

23 You were bought with a price; do not become slaves of men.

1 Corinthians 7:23

Dear God,

Thank You for being my everything.

You set the universe in place.

Who else could do what You have done?

We bow to Your glory and grace.

All nature sings; Hosannas ring. Our God, His glories raise.

Surely You are the wonder of all, and we love to praise Your name.

[10] He was in the world, and the world was made through Him, and the world did not know Him. [11] He came to His own, and those who were His own did not receive Him. [12] But as many as received Him, to them He gave the right to become children of God, *even* to those who believe in His name,

John 1:10-12

[25] Now to Him who is able to establish you according to my gospel and the preaching of Jesus Christ, according to the revelation of the mystery which has been kept secret for long ages past, [26] but now is manifested, and by the Scriptures of the prophets, according to the commandment of the eternal God, has been made known to all the nations, *leading* to obedience of faith; [27] to the only wise God, through Jesus Christ, be the glory forever. Amen.

Romans 16:25-27

²⁴ He rained down manna upon them to eat And gave them food from heaven.

Psalm 78:24

Let a man regard us in this manner, as servants of Christ
and stewards of the mysteries of God.
² In this case, moreover, it is required of stewards that one be found trustworthy.

1 Corinthians 4:1, 2

Dear God,

Painful circumstances drawn without comprehension,

and I trust You, my God, Lord of my life.

You are not only King of Kings, but You are King over me.

I am hurting; please come to me.

Be over me to direct my steps, until I come full face to You again.

Hold me tightly; infuse my mind with Your thoughts through this day.

I cannot breathe without You.

Thank You for supplying my love as manna to pick each morning.

Come for me, circumstances aside.

You are triumph. Honor and glory to You!

You are my great love, and I am Your liege.

[29] My Father, who has given *them* to Me, is greater than all; and no one is able to snatch *them* out of the Father's hand. [30] I and the Father are one."
John 10:30,31

[6] and He has made us *to be* a kingdom, priests to His God and Father— to Him *be* the glory and the dominion forever and ever. Amen.
Revelation 1:6

Dear God,

Distilled moment in us,

Spirit-led to simple understanding in action,

and I am so glad You came to us with gifts.

You see to allow us to join with You,

our radiant Light of Love.

**12 Then Jesus again spoke to them, saying, "I am the Light of the world;
he who follows Me will not walk in the darkness, but will have the Light of life."
John 8:12**

**25 "O righteous Father, although the world has not known You, yet I have known You;
and these have known that You sent Me;
26 and I have made Your name known to them, and will make it known,
so that the love with which You loved Me may be in them, and I in them."**

John 17:25

5 You shall love the LORD your God with all your heart and with all your soul and with all your might.

Deuteronomy 6:5

Dear God,
I love You first; I love You only.
I love You near; I love You far.
I love You close; I love You always.
Forever, You're my Star.

I love You on the rising and the going,
on the becoming and the flowing,
in the here and the now,
on the aft and the bow.
I love You!

² Grace to you and peace from God our Father and the Lord Jesus Christ.

³ Blessed *be* the God and Father of our Lord Jesus Christ,

who has blessed us with every spiritual blessing in the heavenly *places* in Christ,
⁴ just as He chose us in Him before the foundation of the world,
that we would be holy and blameless before Him. In love
⁵ He predestined us to adoption as sons through Jesus Christ to Himself,
according to the kind intention of His will,
⁶ to the praise of the glory of His grace, which He freely bestowed on us in the Beloved.

Ephesians 1:2-6

God be gracious to us and bless us, *And* cause His face to shine upon us— Selah.

² That Your way may be known on the earth, Your salvation among all nations.

³ Let the peoples praise You, O God; Let all the peoples praise You.

⁴ Let the nations be glad and sing for joy;

For You will judge the peoples with uprightness
And guide the nations on the earth. Selah.

Psalm 67:1-4

Dear God,

You tickle me and make me laugh.

You make my heart sing and shine.

All over the world, my joy reverberates,

as You fill my cup with Your sweet love.

⁶ Sarah said, "God has made laughter for me; everyone who hears will laugh with me."

Genesis 21:6

³⁶ While you have the Light, believe in the Light, so that you may become sons of Light."

These things Jesus spoke, and He went away and hid Himself from them.

John 12:36

¹³ But now I come to You; and these things I speak in the world

so that they may have My joy made full in themselves.

John 17:13

Dear God,

I am not here because I have to be; I'm here because I want to be with You.

You are my heart's treasure, my joy of light and sound,

the softness of my being, the tenderness of my years.

You are the strength that has carried me through,

the maturity of my thoughts, and the playfulness of my laugh.

You are the great I AM, and I enter into Your love through Jesus.

I come to You surrendered and happy to know You.

You called Your Spirit to seal me for You. I am stamped and delivered.

I love You.

[8] Who is the King of glory? The Lᴏʀᴅ strong and mighty, The Lᴏʀᴅ mighty in battle.

Psalm 24:8

[9] Just as the Father has loved Me, I have also loved you; abide in My love.

John 15:9

[21] His master said to him, 'Well done, good and faithful slave. You were faithful with a few things, I will put you in charge of many things; enter into the joy of your master.'

Matthew 25:21

⁹ And they *sang a new song, saying, "Worthy are You to take the book and to break its seals; for You were slain, and purchased for God with Your blood *men* from every tribe and tongue and people and nation ¹⁰ "You have made them *to be* a kingdom and priests to our God; and they will reign upon the earth."

Revelation 5:9, 10

Dear God,

"HOLY, HOLY, HOLY *is* THE LORD GOD, THE ALMIGHTY, WHO WAS AND WHO IS AND WHO IS TO COME."

Revelation 4:8b

Blessings, glory, honor, power, and praise to Your Holy name for You are good, kind, and true.

There is no one like You in Heaven or on the Earth.

Glory and honor to Your Holy name for You are the first, the last, the beginning and the end, the Holy One of God.

You deserve honor, power, and glory, and we give this to You.

Help us to obey You as You deserve to be obeyed, and to honor You as You deserve to be honored for Your love is great, oh Creator.

You are worthy of our devoted love because You are the Lamb Who was slain in our place.

We bring You our hearts and sing praises to Your Holy Name forever with You by our side.

We thank You!

Love and Amen,

[11] "Worthy are You, our Lord and our God, to receive glory and honor and power;

for You created all things, and because of Your will they existed, and were created."

Revelation 4:11

Would you like to have a relationship with God?
God loves You so much that He sent His only Son, Jesus to die for You!

16 "For God so loved the world, that He gave His only begotten Son,
that whoever believes in Him shall not perish, but have eternal life.
17 For God did not send the Son into the world to judge the world,
but that the world might be saved through Him.
18 He who believes in Him is not judged; he who does not believe
has been judged already,
because he has not believed in the name of the only begotten Son of God.
19 This is the judgment, that the Light has come into the world,
and men loved the darkness rather than the Light, for their deeds were evil.
20 For everyone who does evil hates the Light,
and does not come to the Light for fear that his deeds will be exposed.
21 But he who practices the truth comes to the Light,
so that his deeds may be manifested as having been wrought in God."
John 3:16-21

Dear God,

I surrender my life to You through Your Son, Jesus, who died for my sins on the cross.

You are Love, and I want to follow Your leadership.

I know I have done wrong against You and people.

I am sorry for all the sins I have committed. Please forgive me for my sins.

I know that I can only be saved to have a new life through You, Jesus,

I know You are alive, and You are the King of Kings.

I love You: Father God, Jesus, and the Holy Spirit, the three in One.

Please help me to follow Your will for my life and to obey Your words in the Bible by Your love.

Please let me live for You.

In the precious name of Jesus, I pray.

Name: _____

Date:_____

[10] The thief comes only to steal and kill and destroy; I came that they may have life, and have *it* abundantly.

John 10:10

If you prayed this prayer for the first time, welcome to the family of God!

Now, the Holy Spirit of Jesus lives inside of you!

It is a wonderful adventure to release your life daily to God through His Son, Jesus.

You will want to read your Bible every day and pray by talking to God.

The Bible instructs us to join a church where the Bible is taught

and God is worshiped through Jesus by the power of the Holy Spirit.

Jesus wants us all to follow His example and be baptized.

May God bless your journey with Jesus!

Where is God? He lives inside of the ones who love Jesus!

[17] pray without ceasing; 1 Thessalonians 5:17

[38] Peter *said* to them, "Repent, and each of you be baptized in the name of Jesus Christ for the forgiveness of your sins; and you will receive the gift of the Holy Spirit.

Acts 2:38

[25] not forsaking our own assembling together, as is the habit of some, but encouraging *one another*; and all the more as you see the day drawing near.

Hebrews 10:25

Dear God,

Please bless and encourage every follower of Jesus so we may be strengthened to do Your will.

Let us honor You through our service to You and others.

Please let many people sincerely love You through our testimony. Your will be done.

In the name of Jesus, I pray.

[9] "Pray, then, in this way:

Our Father who is in heaven,
Hallowed be Your name.
[10] 'Your kingdom come.
Your will be done,
On earth as it is in heaven.
[11] 'Give us this day our daily bread.
[12] 'And forgive us our debts, as we also have forgiven our debtors.
[13] 'And do not lead us into temptation, but deliver us from evil.
[For Yours is the kingdom and the power and the glory forever. Amen.']

Matthew 6:9-13

[19] And my God will supply all your needs according to His riches in glory in Christ Jesus.
Philippians 4:19

Jean Ann Shirey graduated from Baylor University. She worked in the Texas Department of Criminal Justice for 22 years and for the University of Texas Medical Branch–Institutional Division many of those years. Jean Ann has four children and eighteen grandchildren. Jean Ann Shirey wrote *Plum Delight: Poetry Of The Earth*, *The Dance of Monterrey*, *White Hall Baptist Church: The Little Country Church of Your Dreams*, *Trumpet Cloud: Poems Of Jesus*, *Honeymoon In Hawaii*, and *Granny's Garden*. She co-authored *Parallels of Light* with Wallace E. Martin. Jean Ann Shirey writes to give glory to God! John 3:16

⁹ **but just as it is written,** "THINGS WHICH EYE HAS NOT SEEN AND EAR HAS NOT HEARD,
AND *which* HAVE NOT ENTERED THE HEART OF MAN,
ALL THAT GOD HAS PREPARED FOR THOSE WHO LOVE HIM."

1 Corinthians 2:9

Made in the USA
Columbia, SC
02 December 2023